CHRISTMAS
with
Country Living

CHRISTMAS
with
Country Living

Library of Congress Catalog Card Number: 97-68505
ISBN: 0-8487-1613-2
ISSN: 1094-2866
Manufactured in the United States of America
First Printing 1997

We're here for you!
We at Oxmoor House are dedicated to serving you with reliable information that expands your imagination and enriches your life. We welcome your comments and suggestions. Please write us at:

> Oxmoor House, Inc.
> Editor, CHRISTMAS WITH *COUNTRY LIVING*
> 2100 Lakeshore Drive
> Birmingham, AL 35209

To order additional publications, call 1-205-877-6560.

Country Living
Editor-in-Chief: Rachel Newman
Executive Editor: Nancy Mernit Soriano
Managing Editor: Mary R. Roby
Senior Editor/Decorating & Design: Robin Long Mayer
Special Projects Editor: Marylou Krajci
Editor-at-Large: James Cramer
Editor/Home Building & Architecture: Pamela Abrahams
Executive Editor/Food: Lucy Wing
Editor/Food: Joanne Lamb Hayes

Oxmoor House, Inc.
Editor-in-Chief: Nancy Fitzpatrick Wyatt
Senior Homes Editor: Mary Kay Culpepper
Senior Foods Editor: Susan Carlisle Payne
Senior Editor, Editorial Services: Olivia Kindig Wells
Art Director: James Boone

CHRISTMAS WITH *COUNTRY LIVING*
Guest Editors: Richard Kollath, Ed McCann
Editor: Shannon Sexton Jernigan
Assistant Editor: Susan Hernandez Ray
Editorial Assistant: Cecile Y. Nierodzinski
Copy Editors: Keri Anderson, L. Amanda Owens
Associate Art Director: Cynthia R. Cooper
Senior Designer: Melissa Jones Clark
Illustrator: Kelly Davis
Senior Photographers: John O'Hagan, Jim Bathie
Photo Stylist: Linda Baltzell Wright
Production and Distribution Director: Phillip Lee
Associate Production Manager: Theresa L. Beste
Production Assistant: Faye Porter Bonner

Foreword

The Christmas season is a time of ritual, a time of family, and a time of home. For those of us who enjoy country living, the season is also accompanied by an invitation to surround ourselves with timeworn, traditional objects, with an emphasis on natural, beautiful materials.

The time and the energy we spend shopping, wrapping, cooking, and decorating, however, is rewarded by the comfort we find in things both traditional and familiar. Unwrapping tree ornaments, like seeing old friends, can match the joy of unwrapping gifts, and the pleasure of baking a favorite cookie recipe is its own reward.

Christmas with Country Living is our harvest of holidays ideas for decorating, gift giving, and entertaining, and you'll find much to inspire you within these pages. This is, above all, a book of ideas. We've chosen images and projects that reflect the philosophy of *Country Living*, showcasing a mix of the best holiday ideas that have appeared in our magazine.

This year let *Christmas with Country Living* help you usher in the holiday with warmth, with joy, and with confidence.

We welcome the holiday as we wrap the gifts, light the candles, and toast our family and friends. When the last logs in the hearth turn to embers, may the spirit of the holiday envelop you.

Happy holidays.
the editors of *Country Living*

Contents

The Spirit of Christmas

A warm welcome awaits you just beyond the front door. You're home for the holidays.

Flames flare, sparking the tradition of hanging the Christmas greens. Once all the decorating has been completed, each family member hooks a stocking to the mantel. This custom was likely derived from the practice of seventeenth-century Dutch children placing wooden shoes outside their front doors.

Every year the Christmas spirit fills the house with comfort and joy. And when that spirit prevails, there's no place on earth cozier than a wing chair drawn close to the hearth.

Trees are such a central part of Christmas, you needn't limit your home to just one. The trees (above) invite contrast. Just around the corner from a tall evergreen garnished with the customary swags and lights, its perfectly proportioned counterpoint is unadorned but for some feathers and a simple cranberry garland.

Part apparition part icon, this star-crowned Christmas tree embodies the magic and wonder of the season (opposite). In ancient times it was customary to honor evergreens for their ability to live through winter's killing frost. Swathed in tinsel and bright light, this tree is heir to that spirit.

Traditions

From the beginning, custom has been an important part of Christmas celebrations in America.

Towers of fruit epitomize grace and plenty in this authentic vignette of a seventeenth-century Pennsylvania house. Such simplicity still appeals to us. Apples, pears, lemons, pineapples, kumquats, grapes, and oranges are accented with boxwood and ivy and set among a host of lustrous pewter serving pieces. Three hundred years ago, fresh fruits would have been a nearly undreamed-of luxury to offer December guests in most parts of the world. Now, classic American holiday hospitality has come to be symbolized by table-sized trees such as these.

TO CREATE
A Lemon Topiary

This miniature tree blossoms with fragrant whole lemons, pinecones, and laurel.

Illuminating the window of a Maine antiques shop, this holiday accent, suitable for any season, can be fashioned in less than an afternoon.

Begin by purchasing a craft foam cone, a length of chicken wire, and a bundle of florist's picks. To support the weight of the lemons, wrap the length of chicken wire around the cone from the top to the bottom. Nestle the wire-covered cone in a sturdy container, such as the moss-blanketed terra-cotta pot used here.

Gather fresh lemons, laurel leaves, and tiny white-painted pinecones found at craft stores or floral shops. Arrange the lemons on the cone in circular rows, working from the base to the tip and pressing the lemons into the foam with the florist's picks. In the same manner, fill in the tree with pinecones, randomly spacing them among the lemons. For a green flourish, tuck in fresh laurel sprigs, allowing them to fan over the lemons and the pinecones.

Training plants to grow in topiary form originated with the Romans. More recently the Victorians popularized the notion of creating topiaries from wire and filling them with moss, greenery, and flowers.

However their roots are traced, these miniature trees are popular again, brightening today's Christmas tablescapes. Because they are best appreciated at intimate range, place topiaries where they can be enjoyed close up—on sideboards, mantels, or tabletops.

For variety, alter the ingredients. Use an interesting vase, garden accessory, or pottery bowl as a pedestal. Likewise, shop the farmers market or the produce section of the grocery store for other kinds of fruit. Oranges, lady apples, limes, and pomegranates are good candidates. And when it comes to choosing greenery, look no further than your own backyard. Even in the depths of winter, pine, spruce, and nandina—along with those holiday standbys, ivy and holly—are there for the clipping.

Garlands

Like scarves, garlands warm doorframes
and chimney fronts with good cheer.

Luxuriant lengths of freshly pruned boxwood, pine, and fir enhance this home's handsome architecture (opposite). Another reward: They make the whole house smell like Christmas. The practice of decorating with boughs of greenery began in antiquity. It is said that evergreen branches conferred good luck on a home. With the felicitous effects of the garlands shown here, that ancient lore may still be true.

Garlands can be used to accent an interesting feature, or to define the architecture of your home. A cascade of fir surrounds an antique grandfather clock that is tucked away in a small alcove (above).

Yards of dried apple slices strung with whole crab apples grace the kitchen of this 1661 Flushing, New York, home. A handmade twig wreath crowns the center swag. The hub of the home, this authentically equipped kitchen has become the highlight of Christmas decorating for the family who resides here.

Vines of ivy and clusters of holly berries clipped from the winter garden garland a log cabin doorway (left). Cup hooks and florist's wire anchor the greenery to the doorframe. Berried holly clusters and leathery ivy leaves hold their color indoors for about three weeks.

In a traditional holiday gesture, boxwood, magnolia leaves, apples, and a pineapple frame the entry to a Connecticut home built in 1751 (opposite). Kept fresh by cold weather, fruits and greenery will last all season long.

Draped across mantels, curled around doorways, and woven through banisters, holiday garlands are adaptable in shape, appearance, and application. Use wooden florist picks and wire to add clusters of your favorite holiday materials to purchased evergreen roping.

• A collection of antique ornaments and small books (top, opposite) punctuate a garland loosely wound with gold beads and spiked with juniper berries.

• Croton leaves, gilded Brazil nuts, miniature pineapples, and proteas (middle, opposite) hint of the tropics.

• Bundles of cinnamon sticks, dried fruits, rose hips, juniper berries, and pomegranates add fragrant spice to earthy greens (bottom, opposite).

A luscious length of boxwood tumbles down a banister (above). Cotton bolls and branches of magnolia leaves, lit with tiny twinkling lights, add a Southern accent. The newel post is softened with a topknot of magnolia, nandina, holly, and pine.

TO CREATE
A Popcorn Garland

Ropes of crinkly white popcorn settle on the tree like a lacing of snow.

The pride of the Minnesota family who decorated it, this glorious nine-foot spruce is resplendent with thoughtfully acquired antique German and Czech ornaments. To complement their collection, the owners devoted several chilly nights to making popcorn garlands.

Whether pursued in front of an electronic hearth or a real one, making popcorn garlands is one of the holiday's quietly satisfying pleasures. Share that pleasure with family and friends, and the task of stringing enough garlands to swag a lofty evergreen proceeds quickly.

The technique takes only seconds to master. Have bowls full of popped corn at the ready. Thread a medium-fine needle with carpet thread knotted at one end and string the kernels along one by one. Every six inches or so, thread on a fresh cranberry. For contrast, consider making a few all-berry ropes as well.

Corn and cranberries have a holiday significance that extends beyond their appearance on the tree. According to legend, Miles Standish found corn stored by Native Americans that saved Mayflower passengers from starvation during their first winter in what is now Massachusetts. Not far from Plymouth, those same natives were sweetening cooked cranberries with their own maple sugar and enjoying the first known cranberry sauce.

Mantels

Flattered by firelight and a host of decorations, the holiday mantel assumes a glamorous identity.

The focal point of the living room, a masterfully decorated mantel sets a festive tone for the entire room (opposite). The arrangement is elegantly spare and symmetrical on each side of the mirror. Strands of cranberry red beads echo the swags of the stenciled border at the ceiling.

An eye-level view (above) reveals the inventiveness of this grouping. A pint-size boxwood tree growing from a terra-cotta pot conveys a sense of height and presence. Sprigs of white pine, red berries, and abandoned birds' nests lend a fanciful mood.

Carefully orchestrated parts can make a decorative whole. From an emerald-painted mantel (above), an evergreen garland spiked with roses, yarrow, and berries complements a nineteenth-century landscape painting—which, in turn, is topped with greens.

A simple flourish, this boa of mixed greenery (opposite) outlines the mantelpiece of a bedroom fireplace. In its lushness, the unadorned swag suits the room's traditional decor while acknowledging the gracious abundance of the holiday.

TO CREATE
A Eucalyptus Swag & a Bay Laurel Wreath

Familiar kitchen herbs and spices join a pair of summer flowers for a ring around the fireplace.

Dried pomegranates and cinnamon sticks heighten the aroma of a string of eucalyptus leaves. Draping a paneled chimney breast, the swag's stacked form renders a neat contour that enfolds a bushy bay laurel wreath.

To make a similar garland, assemble a quantity of dried eucalyptus leaves, cinnamon sticks, and pomegranates (all are available from floral supply stores). With an electric drill and a ¼" or ¾" bit, drill a small hole through the center of each cinnamon stick and pomegranate.

Using a needle and doubled carpet thread, string a cinnamon stick onto the thread. Carefully work the needle through the center of a stack of bay leaves, one at a time. Top with a pomegranate. Secure with a knot before adding the next stack of bay leaves. Continue the process until the swag is as long as desired.

The laurel wreath, which was purchased plain, is embellished with dried hydrangea and lunaria blooms. These pale flowers dry to a snowy white, a fitting contrast to the dark green bay laurel leaves.

Wreaths

To hang a wreath is to know that the Christmas
season has finally arrived.

Charmed circles grace the
door of a tin-roofed shed in the Catskills.
Three wreaths—one each of eucalyptus,
pepper berry, and dried kochia—are
grouped together as one graphic form
(opposite). Florist's pins hidden in the
greenery fasten them together.

A rectangle of magnolia
takes its shape from an old picture frame
(above). Dozens of stems are bound in
place with waxed florist's twine. A silk bow
suspends the wreath from the picture mold-
ing, making it a stand-in for the painting
that usually hangs over the sideboard.

Crimson pepper berries conceal a small straw base. Berry-laden branches offer dense coverage. A loop of cotton string tied to the base before the berries are glued on forms a hanger for this lightweight wreath.

Woody grapevine tendrils

are ornamented with fruit and foliage
(right). Lady apples, glossy holly, and fiery
berries are attached to the vine wreath with
florist's picks. Leaving part of the form
exposed creates a pleasing visual rhythm.

Crisp, seeded eucalyptus

makes a wreath with an unmistakable
fragrance (right)—and when this wreath is
brought indoors, it releases its exotic fragrance in the warm air. The lush foliage
quickly fashions a large wreath when cuttings are secured with florist's pins to a
straw base.

On a cabin door hangs a traditional ivy-and-berry wreath cinched with a red bow (below) next to an antique homespun blouse. A small woolen bear cradled in the crook of the wreath serves as a reminder of childhood.

A ring of chili peppers holds fast to the latch of a dining room hutch (opposite). With its jaunty raffia hanger, the same wreath could spice up the holiday mood of a kitchen or a breakfast room.

TO CREATE
A Lavender Wreath

A ring of lavender, banked by evergreen boughs, red pomegranates, and large pinecones, invokes a quiet sense of celebration.

To make this simple, fragrant wreath, cut sprigs of lavender in the summer when the flowers are almost three-fourths open. Dry by hanging in small bundles in a dark, arid area. Using a vine wreath as a base, tuck the ends of the bundles into the wreath, separating the vines as needed with a screwdriver. Completely cover the base, filling in holes by hot-gluing sprigs to the wreath.

Lavender's restorative powers have been known for centuries. In ancient Roman times lavender was used in bathwater. The word *lavender* is derived from the Latin *lava,* meaning "to wash." The Romans introduced this plant to Britain, and from then on monks cultivated it in their gardens. During Tudor times lavender was

noted for its aroma and its power to ease stiff joints and to relieve tiredness. In seventeenth-century France, huge fields of lavender were grown for the perfume trade, a practice that continues today. The intoxicating scent can be found in sachets, soaps, potpourri, and perfumes.

For wreath variations, add other dried herbs like baby's breath, rosemary, artemisia, or Mexican sage in the same manner. For additional color, dry roses, carnations, or larkspur in a plastic or glass container filled with a desiccant such as sand, borax, or silica gel. Gently cover the blooms with a layer of desiccant and let them dry for three to four days. Hot-glue clusters of the herbs and the flowers to the base.

Naturals

Of all the presents Christmas brings, nothing is quite as extraordinary as nature's gifts.

Abundant cuttings of rose hip, Fraser fir, pine, and yarrow overflow from a vintage bucket (opposite). While this container charms with its simplicity, a variety of vases would be appropriate for such a spirited holiday arrangement. Vintage tins, baskets or spongeware jugs offer their own artful informality.

Dried pods of *Nigella damascena,* commonly known as love-in-a-mist, reach out from a footed brass pot (above). Whether purchased fresh from a floral shop or clipped from the summer garden, these flowers preserve beautifully. Hang a bunch upside down in a dark room, and they'll dry in less than two weeks.

Grace notes in a spare setting, natural decorations impart a spirit that effortlessly balances elegance and innocence. A wooden swan, carved in New England more than a century ago, is nested in fragrant indigo-berried juniper in a Connecticut dining room. A tin chandelier circled with a ring of fresh ivy and a rope of cranberries hangs over this rustic centerpiece. An indoor garden of narcissus bulbs, planted in a primitive toolbox set on the windowsill, is just coming into flower.

Nature's bounty,

preserved last summer, makes overnight holiday guests welcome in this Connecticut home. A tracery of rose-hip branches twines round the tester of this four-poster bed. Bundles of dried lavender—a flower long believed to possess calming powers—rest on a bedside table to soothe guests to sleep.

Pepper berries drift down from the top of an English wall cupboard (opposite). Clipped from a tree with the leaves intact, the branches require virtually no arranging. A radiant white pillar candle atop an 1800s Italian sconce illuminates the scene.

Twisting stems of rosehips (above), picked from a flower bush still berried in winter, fill a basket handwoven in Maryland. It's often the simplest natural materials without any embellishment, such as these, that make the most delightful Christmas decoration.

Dainty lady apples (below), each a bit larger than a sugarplum, are piled on a platter. Thanks to golden ribbon hangers secured with straight pins, they're ready to trim a kitchen Christmas tree.

As the scene of so many seasonal activities, the kitchen merits a tree all its own (opposite). Decorating the tree with fruit was popularized in the 1600s by the Germans who hung wafers, sweets, and apples on their fir trees at Christmas.

Flowers

As the days grow shorter and winter's chill becomes stronger, brighten your home with blossoms that celebrate the joys of Christmas.

A holiday red amaryllis blooms from a container covered with pinecones (opposite). A colorful cascade of fruits and greens enriches its presentation and camouflages the potting soil.

Perfumed narcissus bulbs, flowering in a wooden box, make a rustic arrangement on the coffee table (above). A ribbon bow supports these tall flowers, keeping potentially wayward stems upright.

As familiar as a carol, a scarlet poinsettia declares that Christmas has come to the parlor (opposite). Euphorbia poinsettia is a native of Mexico; its holiday popularity there intrigued Joel Roberts Poinsett, the first U.S. ambassador to the country. In 1825 the cuttings he sent to his greenhouses in South Carolina created such a sensation that a nurseryman in Philadelphia eventually named the plant in Poinsett's honor.

In his journals, Poinsett called poinsettias "flame leaves." Modern hybrids run the spectrum from crimson to chartreuse. Making the most of several shades, a colorful sampling of small potted poinsettias (above) animates a foyer.

Creamy white tulips

burst from a spray of pine and berries
on a mantel. A gingerbread mold and
a teapot flank the pewter pitcher.
Fruits, nuts, pinecones, and greenery
soften the shelf. When purchasing
tulips this holiday season, buy them
in bud—they'll last longer.

Cranberry red tapers spark this one-of-a-kind living room chandelier crafted by an artisan from tin and an antique table leg.

Christmas Glow

The subtlety of candlelight kindles the mystery
and the magic of Christmas.

Snowy white votive candles are spiked with dark brown cloves (above). When the wicks are lit, the spicy scent is enticing. To stud a purchased candle, use the hot tip of a glue gun to melt the wax enough to lightly press in each clove.

Alight in ivory, the walkway of this Connecticut home reprises the Mexican custom of lighting luminarias outdoors on Christmas Eve (below). The decorations are simple to duplicate: Fill small white paper bags about one-third full of sand and place a candle in each one. Make certain, though, not to position luminarias too close to grass, flowers, or shrubbery and don't light them on windy days.

The flickering light from a half-dozen votive candles casts a golden spell on whitewashed cupboard shelves (opposite). The beauty of these lights—and their nondescript glass holders—lies in their versatility. Arranged in groups, they add a glow to dining tables, mantels, and coffee tables.

Trees

Spirits leap when the tree goes up, for it is the soul
of Christmas at home.

The search is on every year to find the perfect tree that stretches from floor to ceiling, has neither bare spots nor needle drop, and smells precisely like an enchanted forest. Happily, the annual hunt almost always yields something near the ideal—once the tree is decorated. On the sturdy boughs of a Scotch pine (opposite), cookie wreaths are hung with red satin bows. For cookie ornament recipes, see pages 130 and 134.

A verdant backdrop for heartfelt trimmings, a Christmas tree conjures up happy memories. This eclectic assortment of handcrafted ornaments and glass balls, collected through the years, graces a small fir tree (above).

Green canvases for family treasures, three regal trees bank this cottage corner with spicy-smelling greenery. Each is carefully decked with construction-paper chains, big-bulb lights, and brand-new ornaments that look as if they've been in the family forever.

TO CREATE

A Tree Skirt and Stocking

Dimensional holly leaves and berries trim this snowy
white wool tree skirt and matching stocking.

Cut a 62″ square from the cream wool. Fold the square in half and then in half again to mark the center. Unfold the square.

Make a compass by tying a pencil to one end of the string; measure 30" of the string and tie a pushpin into the other end. Stick the pushpin in the center of the wool and draw a 60"-diameter circle. Measure 3" of string and draw a 6"-diameter circle in the center of the 60" circle. Cut out the outer circle. Cut a straight line from the outer edge to the inner circle for the skirt opening; cut out the inner circle.

Trim the edges with the pinking shears. Turn all of the raw edges under ⅝" to the wrong side and steam-press. Insert the cording in the fold of the outer hem. Using the zipper foot, topstitch the hem from the wrong side, close to the cording. Topstitch the edges of the opening.

Transfer the leaf pattern to the cardboard, adding a ¼" seam allowance, and cut it out. Transfer the pattern to the remaining cream wool with the water-soluble marker and cut 19 leaves. Using a blanket stitch and the green thread, machine-stitch around the outer edge of each leaf, gently stretching the wool while stitching to create wavy edges on the leaves. Trim any excess wool close to the stitching.

Cut out circles slightly bigger than the buttons from the cranberry wool. Make a running stitch close to the edge of one wool circle and place a corresponding button in the center. Pull the thread tight to cover the button; fasten it off securely. Repeat to cover all of the buttons.

Spread the tree skirt faceup on a flat surface. Arrange and pin the leaves around the outer edge of the skirt. Referring to the pattern, draw a vein and a coiled stem for each leaf with the water-soluble marker. For each leaf, place a length of tapestry yarn over the marked

Tree Skirt

What you will need:

Patterns on page 155

1¾ yards 60"-wide cream wool coating

⅝ yard 60"-wide ecru wool coating

1 yard string

Pencil

Pushpin

Pinking shears

7 yards ³⁄₁₆"-diameter cording

Lightweight cardboard

Water-soluble marker

⅛ yard medium-weight cranberry wool

Sewing thread: green, cream

Buttons: 13 (¾"), 18 (⅝"), 18 (½")

White wool tapestry yarn

Tapestry needle

line, leaving 2" extra at each end to pull through to the wrong side. With a cording foot, stitch the yarn to the leaf and the skirt with a zigzag stitch, using the green thread and leaving long thread tails to pull through to the wrong side. At each end, thread the yarn and the thread in the tapestry needle and pull through to the wrong side. Fasten off the thread; trim the yarn ends to ½".

Arrange and pin the berries on the skirt. Stitch the berries to the skirt from the wrong side with the cream thread; fasten them off securely.

Stocking

What you will need:

Patterns on pages 155—157
1 yard 60"-wide cream wool coating
Tracing paper
Water-soluble marker
Lightweight cardboard
16" square ecru wool coating
⅓ yard medium-weight cranberry wool
Buttons: 6 (¾"), 18 (⅝"), 8 (½")
Thread: cream, green, cranberry

Lightly felt the cream wool by washing it and then drying it on high heat. Use the tracing paper and the water-soluble marker to transfer the stocking pattern to the cream wool.

Cut one stocking; reverse the pattern and cut another.

Follow leaf instructions for the tree skirt to make six leaves from the ecru wool.

With the right sides facing and the raw edges aligned, use a ¼" seam allowance and stitch the two stockings pieces together along the toe side and around the toe only. Fasten off and press the seam open.

Arrange six leaves on the front of the stocking. Repeat for the back of the stocking. Pin them to secure. Use the water-soluble marker to mark the stems and the veins of the leaves.

Beginning near the tip of one leaf and following the marked line, use the green thread and a zigzag stitch to stitch the leaf to the stocking. Continue stitching the line past the base of the leaf to create the stem. Repeat with the remaining leaves. (For leaves that overlap the unstitched heel side seam of the stocking, embroider the stem but attach each leaf to the stocking after the heel side seam is stitched.)

Follow berry instructions for the tree skirt to make three ¾", nine ⅝", and four ½" berries. Using the cranberry thread, handstitch the berries to the stocking. With the right sides facing and the raw edges aligned, stitch the stocking front and back together along the heel side seam. Refer to the leaf instructions above to stitch any leaves that overlap the back seam.

For the stocking cuff, cut one 9" x 17" rectangle from the cranberry wool. With the right sides facing and the raw edges aligned, fold the rectangle in half widthwise. Using a ¼" seam allowance, stitch the 9" ends together; turn. With the wrong sides facing, fold the cuff in half lengthwise.

Pin the stocking top inside the cuff, aligning the raw edges at the top. Using a ¼" seam allowance, machine-stitch the cuff to the stocking through all the thicknesses. Press the seam allowance toward the stocking. Edgestitch the stocking top, catching the cuff seam allowance.

For the hanger, cut one 1½" x 6" rectangle from the remaining cranberry wool. With the right sides facing and the raw edges aligned, fold the rectangle in half lengthwise. Using a ¼" seam allowance, machine-stitch the 6" ends together; turn and press. Fold the tube in half; align the raw edges with the cuff raw edges inside the stocking at the heel side seam and stitch.

Feather Trees

Artifice and ingenuity meet in one of Germany's most decorative gifts to the season.

By Mary R. Roby

"A tree made of feathers!" my mother exclaimed in disbelief when she opened my present to her a couple of Christmases ago.

Since then, she has grown to cherish her little tabletop tree. As the holidays approach, she retrieves it from its storage corner in the closet, bends down its wire branches, and dresses them with the miniature heart-shaped gingerbread cookies and blown-glass ornaments contributed by my sister Carol and me. The little tree never fails to instill the Christmas spirit in my mother's living room, and decorating it beats having to grapple with a six-foot conifer.

Although feather trees no longer dominate yuletide parlors, these delicate arbors still capture imagination. A 1912 Marshall Field & Co. advertisement enticed readers with this description: "Christmas Trees Made of Feathers. Branches Stout and Heavy with Many Side Twigs, with Candle Holders and Red Berries." The ad illustrates a perfectly symmetrical tree, likely imported from Germany, standing in a "painted wooden pot."

Made in Germany

Germans have always celebrated Christmas with gusto, and beginning in the 1870s they started to manufacture most of the tree ornaments and other holiday decorations prized by today's collectors. In the 1890s a resourceful and innovative soul hit upon the idea of creating an artificial "evergreen" by using feathers as a folksy replica for real pine needles.

"From what can be determined, feather tree manufacturing was a cottage industry similar to the manufacture of glass Christmas ornaments," Robert Brenner writes in *Christmas Past* (Schiffer Publishing Ltd., 1985). "However, it was different in several respects. The parts for the tree—wire, wood, and berries—were factory made." According to Brenner, workers wrapped the heavy wire branches with feathers, usually from turkeys or geese, although swan feathers were also used at times. Generally the feathers were dyed a dark green, giving the branches a natural and appealing look.

Feather Trees Travel to America

Compact, easy-to-store feather trees first arrived in this country with German immigrants. Collapsible wire branches reduced the tree to a slim, feathery pole for easy storage, convenient for tucking into a steamer trunk. Most of the trees that traveled to America were probably suitable for tabletops, measuring about 2½ to 3 feet high, a size popular in Germany in the late nineteenth century. The nostalgic yearnings felt by the newcomers at holiday time could be somewhat eased by retrieving the tree from storage, bending down its branches, and adorning them with little ornaments.

Turn-of-the-century magazines helped spread the popularity of feather trees. An article in the December 1900 issue of *Harper's Bazaar* tells of a small Nuremberg Christmas tree decorating the center of the table at a children's dinner.

Soon department stores and mail-order catalogs offered the trees. For instance, the 1913 Sears, Roebuck and Co. catalog advertised artificial trees in four sizes ranging from 17 inches high and 11 inches wide to 55 inches high and 34 inches wide. The large size had an easy-to-store, two-part trunk.

The Market Expands

German imports ceased during both world wars, but consumers could continue to purchase trees in department stores and through catalogs during the 1920s and 1930s.

Although the feather trees did adhere to a basic form—plumed branches inserted into a central wooden pole with a supporting base—the details varied. For instance, the wooden base could be cylindrical or square. Earlier trees sported round bases painted red or white, sometimes embellished with a gold band. Later examples were planted in square bases decorated with stenciled holly designs. In the 1930s, Germans also experimented with different colors for the feathers, ranging from dark to light green. Some of the branches even had shaded ends and were finished with blue or white berries, rather than the traditional red. After the 1940s, consumers could also buy white trees as well as royal blue models with red-tipped branches.

Some trees had fewer branches, producing a spare look, while others had as many as one branch for every inch of tree height. Before the Second World War, trees with built-in electric lights became available.

Favor of Feather Trees

In the 1930s, the invention of cellophane signaled the feather tree's fall from favor. After the Second World War, boughs of wired crepe and Visca, a dark green straw-like rayon, entered the artificial tree marketplace, dimming the demand for feather trees still further. By the 1950s, most stores and catalogs no longer sold them.

However, the feather tree may have disappeared from the marketplace for Christmas decorations, but its absence was only a temporary one. In the 1970s, interest in American folk art and vintage holiday decorations began to soar, and feather trees again became a part of the holiday scene. Today, vintage feather trees are scarce and are, therefore, quite expensive, averaging as much as $100 per foot or more, depending on the condition.

Miniature Trees

A host of charming little trees present all sorts of possibilities
for holiday decorating and gift-giving.

A weathered watering can cradled in a blanket of moss doubles as a tree stand for the trimmed top branches of a small cedar (opposite). Spun-cotton pears, crafted in the late 1800s, hang from the greens.

An arrangement of evergreen branches enhanced by small scale ornaments brims from a whitewashed wooden pail (above). Keep the clippings from a big Christmas tree to fashion this whimsical smaller version.

Like snowflakes, sprigs of Queen Anne's lace settle upon the branches of a dwarf Alberta spruce (top, left). The tree is nestled inside a nineteenth-century wallpaper-covered hatbox.

A painted canoe from the 1930s carries small cypress and spruce trees decorated with pinecones, baby's breath, and miniature mittens (bottom, left).

Watched over by an angel, a balled-in-burlap fir glistens with sparkling clay icicle ornaments (opposite). After the holidays, a live tree can be planted and enjoyed for years.

TO CREATE
Mossy Trees for a Tabletop

Cones wrapped in velvety coats make for everlasting evergreens.

When a Christmas tree's traditional form is reduced to its essence—as it is here—the result is seasonal sculpture. These handmade topiaries rise tall from terra-cotta pots to oversee the holiday bustle in a cozy log cabin. Lean and graceful, the trees reiterate this room's spareness, though they are well suited to a variety of decorative styles.

To make a tree of your own, gather the necessary materials: plaster of Paris, a large stick for the trunk, a terra-cotta pot, a craft foam cone, florist's tape, spray adhesive, and sheet moss. Also have on hand a plastic bucket that can be concealed in the pot. Be sure to work on a protected surface.

Mix the plaster of Paris according to the package directions. Quickly pour the plaster mixture into the plastic bucket. Before the plaster hardens, insert the stick trunk into the center of the bucket; hold the trunk upright with a brace of florist's tape until the plaster completely hardens.

Coat the top surface of the cone with spray adhesive. Press small, easy-to-manage pieces of sheet moss onto the adhesive-coated area. Once the top is covered, spray the adhesive on the bottom of the cone and wrap the remaining area with moss.

Assemble the tree by pressing the bottom of the cone onto the top of the trunk. Conceal the plaster with sheet moss. Place the tree in the terra-cotta pot.

Embellish the tree—or not—according to your taste. You might wind a strand of wooden beads around the cone, invisibly securing the thread every so often with straight pins. Dried vine or French wired ribbon would also make an appropriate garland. Small ornaments, whose delicacy would be lost on a larger tree, surely come into their own at this diminutive scale.

Spruce saplings, bound in burlap and topped with gilded Moravian Stars, evoke the dignity of their larger siblings. This little grove, destined for gift-giving, sits ready on a buffet. To mimic this wrapping, place a waterproof saucer on a large unfinished square of burlap. Set a tree, still in its nursery pot, onto the saucer. Gather the burlap around the pot and tie it in place with a ribbon bow. Then top with a star.

Collections

Souvenirs of another time and place, antique Christmas keepsakes help us preserve cherished traditions.

Hand-blown ornaments rest weightlessly on the branches of a Christmas tree (opposite). Shaped to resemble pinecones, gingerbread houses, bells, and icicles, these fantasies in glass radiate shimmering color.

Peeking out from evergreen needles, golden German and Czech baubles dress the tree with an old-fashioned flair (above). A beaming Pierrot ornament mingles with a tinseled chromolithograph angel and a picture postcard of Santa.

Vintage Christmas Tree Ornaments

Luminosity is the most captivating feature of nineteenth-century glass ornaments.

By Mary Seehafer Sears

As you hang ornamental glass balls on your Christmas tree this year, you'll be repeating a ritual begun more than one hundred years ago in Germany.

For decades, the glassblowing business was centered primarily in the Thuringian Forest region, near Germany's center. German glassblowers and their families first made festive glass globes, called *Kugeln,* as an offshoot to their production of glass toys, glass eyes, and other glass items.

The earliest ornaments were either hand blown or made using molds. In addition to round balls, manufacturers produced bells, horns, and tree toppers, known as *Piken,* or points. Fruit-shaped ornaments were particularly popular. Delicate ornaments with spun-glass trimmings and "skirts," glass icicles, and strings of ornamental glass beads became part of the glassblower's art, too.

While some *Kugeln* were made simply of clear or colored glass, most had silver interiors for a metallic glow. Still others caught the eye with decorated swirls, stars, and circular patterns; others were spotted with colored wax. Some ornaments were dipped in lacquer.

These early ornaments were first made to adorn the wooden crowns that many German families hung from the ceilings of their homes during the holiday season, which were evocative of Christ's Crown of Thorns. The crown had its counterparts in Victorian England where kissing boughs were hung from the ceiling and decorated with mistletoe, ribbons, apples, and lit candles.

It's impossible to know when the first Christmas tree was erected. Some of the earliest German trees were tabletop size. Immigrants carried this idea, and their glassblowing skills, across the ocean to America. In 1891, President Benjamin Harrison had the first full-size Christmas tree in the White House, and the idea caught on.

Handcrafted Ornaments

A dizzying variety of handmade decorations adorned the first Christmas trees. Heavily laden boughs offered edibles such as cookies, candy, citrus fruits like oranges and tangerines, and walnuts dipped in egg whites and wrapped in gold foil. Paper chains festooned branches as well. Swedes hung straw animal figures, Czechs painted eggshells, and Danes made paper hearts and bells.

Ornaments in Shapes

Fruit and vegetable ornaments eventually replaced their real-life complements on trees. Grapes and pinecones were particularly popular. Grapes were a symbol of plenty, and pinecones symbolized both motherhood and fertility. Realistic apple and nut-shaped ornaments were hung alongside more fanciful shapes such as bananas, corn, watermelons, and pickles.

The pickle ornament was often the object of a German hide-and-seek game on Christmas morning. When the tree was decorated on Christmas Eve, *Mutter und Vater* would hide the pickle ornament among the branches. The first child to spot the pickle on Christmas morning would receive a special prize.

Other popular ornaments depicted birds, soldiers, trumpets, coffeepots, angels, houses and cottages, churches, doghouses, and skinny, dour Santa Clauses (Santa Claus didn't look jolly until 1822, when Clement Moore wrote *A Visit from St. Nicholas* in 1863, and German-born American editorial cartoonist Thomas Nast gave Santa the cheerful countenance we know today). Shiny "scrap pictures" called chromolithographs, were also affixed to glass ornaments for export to this country.

Homemade Ornaments

In his compendium of Christmas tree history, *The Christmas Tree Book*, Phillip V. Snyder tells how F. W. Woolworth, in search of Christmas goods for his dime-store customers, traveled to Germany in 1890 to place orders with glassblowers. In 1880, when he first saw the glass ornaments at a Philadelphia importing firm, Woolworth was uncertain whether these feather-light ornaments would be popular with his customers (he feared the ornaments might be too fragile for them), so he decided to place a modest order. Astonished

when the baubles sold out, he placed a far heftier order the following year.

An American Industry Born

American imitations of German ornaments were being sold in this country as early as 1919, but their quality could not match that of the German imports, such as those brought into this country by German-born Max Eckardt in the 1920s. As the Second World War approached, importation became impossible, and Eckardt switched his production to the Corning Glass Works in Corning, New York. Corning had been making ornaments experimentally on their light-bulb machines. In a joint venture begun in 1939 that proved highly successful, the first Corning-made clear-glass globes were sent to Eckardt's company in New Jersey for decorating. In no time, it seemed every tree in America was glowing with glass balls.

Machine-made decorations produced in American factories soon became the norm. The small home-operated, family-run businesses that characterized the early German industry could no longer compete.

Collectors on the Search

Today, old-fashioned hand-blown ornaments are much in demand and are often handed down from generation to generation. At Kelter-Malcé, an antiques store in New York City, hand-blown ornaments sell for $35 to $350 apiece, depending on their complexity. Canny collectors can search antiques shops and estate sales around the country, occasionally uncovering these gems of yesteryear.

Family heirlooms bridge the past with the present and speak of a time yet to come when these objects may grace our children's homes.

A collection of playthings that once sparked a child's imagination now captures the fancy of grown-ups. There is still a beguiling sweetness to the worn fur, the fragile limbs, and the amiable expressions of the toys. These tell the tales of Christmases past (opposite page, clockwise from top left): Sheep with tattered coats remain soft to the touch; a timeworn wooden hobby-horse wears a ribbon-and-holly corsage; and grinning clowns and a bareback rider—sprung from the imagination of a Philadelphia toymaker in the early 1900s—cavort anew.

Handstitched features are the telling signs of a well-made plush toy. This puppy's nose and mouth (above) are carefully sewn below shining glass eyes. His frayed tie frames a lovable face.

A stylish fellow in a bright yellow cardigan and a gray felt hat (above) recalls the teddy bear's forefather, President Theodore Roosevelt. According to one story, Roosevelt was hunting in Mississippi when he came across a baby black bear. The animal was too adorable for him to shoot and, thus, was nicknamed "Teddy's Bear." In 1906 a clever toymaker introduced a plush bear that capitalized on the tale. The toy quickly became all the rage, an American passion that continues today.

Loved to pieces, faithful bears like these (opposite) bring out the kid in toy collectors. The kind faces of these childhood classics spark nostalgia for holidays past. Whether displayed among the gifts under the tree or set on a tabletop with other collections, these furry friends warrant an appearance every Christmas.

Collectible Santas, in their many manifestations, are perhaps the season's most coveted treasures. A jolly 1920s Saint Nick (center) extends his arms with glad tidings. On each side of him, blue-coated gentlemen represent the gruff Belsnickle character who visited German children on Christmas Eve. Other Santas in this group bear flags, lanterns, evergreens, and good wishes for the holiday.

AN ESSAY

Santa Claus: A Man with a Past

By Carol Cook Hagood

Long before the jolly old soul became the North Pole's most celebrated resident, he was bringing gifts to the poor in Asia Minor.

Everyone loves Santa, but no one more than my friend Mary. Mary collects Santa figures, prints, trays, tins, and memorabilia. Over the years, starting with a few small chalk figurines picked up at a country flea market, she's assembled an impressive crowd of Clauses, each with a different face and form. During the holidays, Mary's Santas line the mantel, fill the bookshelves, circle the tree, and gaze out from her tabletop centerpiece. They form a festive army that grows larger with every season, as friends surprise her with intriguing new finds.

It's a pleasant passion Mary has, one she shares with a growing number of collectors. Santa figures can be found in many shapes and sizes and are made of materials as different as papier-mâché, cloth, ceramic, celluloid, cardboard, and tin. In many collections, modern-day folk-art Santas mingle easily with fading collectibles from decades past and from around the world.

For those of us who grew up with the plump and jolly wrapping-paper Santas of the American fifties and sixties, the most collectible—the tall, stern Father Christmases, the brooding Belsnickles—seem worlds apart from our childhood notions. They hint at a long history full of different ideas about the generosity at the heart of the holiday season. And, indeed, that is the case as it is so vividly portrayed in the brilliant biography *The Santa Claus Book* by E. Willis Jones (Walker and Company, 1976).

A Wonderful History

As *The Santa Claus Book* notes, the story of Santa Claus is a very old one. It begins many hundreds of years ago in Asia Minor with the original Saint Nicholas, a fourth-century bishop of the seaport town of Myra on the Mediterranean. Nicholas, we are told, was a devout youngster, the only child of wealthy parents who adored him. When his parents died suddenly in a plague, the nine-year-old Nicholas used his family's riches to help others who were poor and in need or who, like him, found their world shaken by an unexpected turn of events.

The most famous instance of charity concerns an elderly nobleman, a friend of Nicholas's family, who had lost his fortune. His three beautiful daughters were unable to marry, although each had a suitor, because the father could not provide them with the traditional dowries. Worse still, the daughters were considering a desperate step: drawing lots to decide which one of them would sell herself in order to keep the struggling family afloat.

When young Nicholas learned of this terrible situation, he took a small round bag of gold and, in the dark of night, tossed the gold through the oldest daughter's window. The gold fell and lodged, some say, in one of her stockings left hanging up to dry. In turn, two more bags of gold, secretly given by Nicholas, rescued the younger sisters as well.

A Friend to Many

Many of the miraculous stories about Saint Nicholas involve ships and sailors. Once, to save his seaport town from famine, Bishop Nicholas persuaded some ships' captains to share grain from their cargoes, assuring them that their generosity would be rewarded. When the ships arrived at their destination, sailors were astonished to find their storage bins completely full and overflowing, despite the stores they had shared.

Because of this and other seagoing miracles, Nicholas in time became the patron saint of sailors—as well as of many other diverse groups, including spinsters, little children, all Russians, New York City, bankers, and pawnbrokers. (Remember young Nicholas's three bags of gold? They reappear as the three golden balls found on almost every pawnbroker's storefront.)

The Legend Spreads

During the centuries that followed, sailors spread stories of their patron Saint Nicholas throughout Europe, and Saint Nicholas reappeared in various guises in many countries. It may be that the practice of leaving gifts at the homes of poor children on December 5, Saint Nicholas's Eve, was begun by twelfth-century French nuns. At any rate, over the years, giving gifts in the name of Saint Nicholas became a common custom on Saint

Nicholas's Eve. In many places, the evening was also marked by a festive parade, featuring an appearance by "Saint Nicholas" dressed in red bishop's robes and a mitered hat and carrying a shepherd's crook.

In some areas, the kindly Saint Nicholas was accompanied on his gift-giving rounds by a frightful servant known as Rumpaus, Krampas, or Hansruhpart. He scared the children, warning them against bad behavior, before Saint Nicholas stepped in to hand out the presents. In certain parts of Germany, Saint Nicholas himself, called *Pelze Nicol* (Nicholas in fur) or Belsnickle, appeared as the servant to Krist Kindl—the Christ Child—represented by a young child dressed in white with a crown of glowing candles. (This association eventually led to Santa's sometimes being called Kris Kringle.)

In time, the various legends of Saint Nicholas came to America, brought by European immigrants to the New World. Of these, no group was more fond of the old stories and the old saint than the Dutch who settled New Amsterdam (later to become New York). They called him Sinterklaas and celebrated his day on December 6 with home-baked treats and surprise gifts delivered by the saint on the evening of December 5. When Washington Irving published *Knickerbocker's History of New York* in 1809, his affectionate and humorous look at Dutch customs included a description of Santa as a red-clad, behatted, pipe-smoking elf. This is the first description of the saint by a well-known American writer.

An American Hero

Then, in 1822, one of the most inspired versions of the Santa Claus story was written by Clement Moore, who read Irving's book and used it as a starting point for *A Visit from St. Nicholas,* also known as *The Night*

Before Christmas. Originally conceived as Christmas Eve entertainment for his family, Moore's poem has become a holiday classic, with enormous impact on Americans' image of Santa.

Still later, the legendary political cartoonist Thomas Nast—who is also credited with creating the GOP elephant and the Democrat donkey—read Moore's ode and did a series of Santa pen-and-inks for *Harper's Weekly* in 1863. These drawings depict a tall, round, bearded gentleman who is merrily smoking a pipe, wearing a red suit and a matching hat trimmed with white fur.

Other famous illustrators played their part in the transformation of Saint Nicholas from the tall, thin cleric of European legend to the jolly, rotund, white-bearded Santa Claus. Norman Rockwell, for one, produced covers for the *Saturday Evening Post* in the 1920s, showing a grandfatherly Santa supervising his elves or studying the globe as he plans worldwide visits. None,

however, have been more important in fixing the image of a plump, jovial, lovable old elf than Haddon Sundblom, an advertising artist who also created other icons of American commercial art. Beginning in 1931 and continuing for decades after, Sundblom's holiday ads for Coca-Cola featured a warm, robust, and jolly Santa Claus who, for many, embodies the joyfulness and festivity of the holiday.

My friend Mary's collection includes several vintage tin trays featuring Coca-Cola Santas. I take them down from her shelf and enjoy them anew, marveling at the warm colors, the rich detail, the hearty smiles of this favorite-of-many Santa. Then I pick up, in turn, several of her small Santa figures, with their curious expressions, their half-told tales of Christmases past. It's no wonder that so many treasure these little messengers. Each, in his own way, tells again of the joyful spirit of giving that once, long ago, sent the boy Nicholas out into the night with a secret gift of gold.

Muslin ornaments, these snowmen (opposite and above) are wrapped with wool mufflers. Their cloth bodies are stuffed with batting to different proportions, giving each its own identity. Tea-dyed cotton snowballs and a scrap fabric garland add more homespun appeal. A group of handcrafted Santas pose around the Christmas tree.

Stalwart snowmen (below) preside over a mantel shelf. Bottle-brush trees and miniature igloos bask in the yellow glow of a string of tiny white lights. The backdrop—a hunter green construction-paper forest—adds depth in an amusing way. And a skinny swag of marshmallows strung with raisins sweetly underlines the scene.

Paper cherubs hover over a painted mantel (below), blessing the contents of a skinny pair of knitted stockings. Angels like these would have been ornaments for the tree when they were made in Germany in the 1890s. Grouped with other Christmas ephemera, as they are in this arrangement, the angels are even more prominent.

A tin angel sounds her trumpet on a candlelit bookshelf (opposite). For dramatic effect, highlight a single element of a collection with flowers or greenery; sprigs of baby's breath nestle here at the angel's feet.

Taking flight up a log cabin wall, this host of handmade angels (opposite) wears weathered wooden wings made of architectural fragments. These heavenly beauties—enchanted rag dolls, really—are dressed in vintage christening gowns. Wide-eyed embroidered expressions give each one personality.

Thirteen lucky lady apples queue up in a miniature corner cupboard (above), brightening the dark wooden shelves. Even at this diminutive scale, repetition effectively attracts attention.

A child's cabinet holds a toy spongeware tea set (below) with matching plates. The festive little arrangement is outfitted with holly leaves and clove-studded oranges.

Decorating a setting makes ordinary items seem extraordinarily suited for the season (opposite). A collection of lavender-and-white ironstone is dressed for Christmas with embellishments of cedar boughs and lady apples.

Designed for display, the cupboard is a logical place for Christmas decorating. A repainted hutch shelters a fine collection of pottery bowls (opposite). Pine, holly, and lady apples graciously bring the season into the kitchen.

Red-orange bittersweet stems and tiny feather trees embellished with little candles visually unite the varied contents of a rustic server (above). These holiday flourishes bring seasonal color to your favorite collections.

Quick Holiday Ideas

Just in the nick of time, here are eleventh-hour ways
to make the whole house merry.

A peck of marzipan peaches coated
with colored sugar and silver dragées
sparkles in a bowl (opposite). Bowls full of
Christmas cookies or holiday spices make
festive alternatives.

A twig kissing ball sways on
French ribbon suspended from a chair
(above). Cover a purchased twig ball with
gold spray paint and wrap it with elastic
thread strung with tiny beads.

Pear candles, nut ornaments, evergreens, and baby hemlocks in terra-cotta pots add an instant holiday touch to the vintage Irish pine hutch (above). To keep the trees fresh all season, add a cover of sphagnum moss at the base of the baby hemlocks to prevent them from drying out.

Gilded nut ornaments have a simple, organic beauty (opposite). To make one, hot-glue acorns, chestnuts, beechnuts, and hickory nuts in their shells to a craft foam sphere and coat with spray paint. Keep in mind that the size of the form will double when the nuts are added.

Sprigs of boxwood on each pane (opposite) emulate the tradition of putting candles in the window. Dabs of warm beeswax, kneaded with the fingers, harden to hold sprigs in place.

A swag of Fraser fir, green grapes, and pears tied with satin ribbon (above) presents an alternative to the customary wreath. A length of florist's wire binds the fresh trio together.

Pomanders and glass ornaments fill a china bowl atop a desk (above). This quick decoration, with its wintry scent and shiny glamour, inspires the spirit of the season as you write Christmas cards.

A vast collection of apothecary jars elegantly displays holiday candy (opposite). Since the candy might not last very long, consider replacing it with colorful miniature glass ornaments.

Decorative Scents

Heighten the evergreen fragrance of Christmas with the subtle aromas of fresh herbs, dried flowers, and homemade potpourri.

Lavender flowers and assorted colors of rose petals create a romantic Christmas mix. To make potpourri sachets, wrap the mixture in pieces of mesh material and secure with satin ribbons. Hang the sachets on a Christmas tree (opposite) by the loops to add to the fragrance of the holidays.

For a heavenly sweet-scented potpourri (above), mix one cup of lavender flowers, eight cups of dried rose petals, one tablespoon of ground cloves, four drops of rose oil, and two tablespoons each of ground allspice, ground cinnamon, and ground orrisroot. Seal in an airtight container for six weeks before packaging.

A leisurely walk outdoors can turn up the ingredients for a woodsy potpourri. Combine two cups of cedar bark shavings, one cup of sandalwood shavings, two tablespoons of orrisroot powder, five drops of cedar wood oil, and three cups of cedar twigs, small pinecones, and juniper berries. Mix well. Place in a sealed container for six weeks before giving.

TO CREATE
Rosemary Trees

Topiaries sculpted from rosemary grow
ready for holiday decorating.

While training these shapely trees takes some time and patience, the rewards are both spectacular and long lasting. To create the ring-shaped topiary, start with a wire wreath frame. Cover the bottom of a pot with a layer of pebbles and top with soil. Press the ends of the frame into the soil. Place two rooted rosemary cuttings on each side of the wire and cut the main tips. About every inch that the rosemary grows, tie it to the wire with raffia and clip the sides for fullness until the two sides meet at the top.

To design the globe-shaped or conical topiary, plant a straight-rooted cutting of rosemary in a pot of sterile, prepackaged soil. Place a bamboo or cane stake in the soil by the plant. Loosely secure the plant to the stake with twist ties or raffia. For the globe-shaped topiary, as the plant grows and its base thickens, pinch off all but the top stems to yield a trunk. When the plant reaches the desired height, control the shape by trimming the top tuft of stems to encourage a rounded, bushy form. Fashioning a conical topiary is simpler: Clip the branches of a medium-sized plant into that familiar Christmas tree shape.

Once you've grown your topiaries, maintenance is easy. Keep them in the sunlight, turning every few days for an even growth. Keep plants moist but be sure not to overwater them. If you're short on time this year, purchase a ready-grown topiary from the local garden center and follow these easy care tips.

Food Gifts to Make

As traditions go, spending time in the kitchen merrily cooking presents for family and friends is one of the happiest.

A wagonload of gift "baskets" filled with pantry fancies is wheeled through the snow (opposite). Jars of spicy-sweet mustard, pomegranate-onion marmalade, and cranberry-kumquat relish fill a pail. The hatbox carries pinwheel cookies and a hive-topped jar of apricot spread.

A fitting container makes for a comely presentation. Throughout the year collect boxes, baskets, and buckets to hold your holiday kitchen creations. Then let the container guide the gift to its recipient; the hatbox (above) was chosen for an avid rose gardener.

Pomegranate-Onion Marmalade

Grenadine syrup and pomegranate seeds color and flavor this onion relish, a flavorful accompaniment to roast meats, baked ham, or meat pâtés.

Makes 2 cups.

2 tablespoons olive oil

2 pounds sweet Spanish onions, sliced

½ teaspoon salt

¼ teaspoon ground white pepper

¾ cup white wine

½ cup honey

¼ cup red wine vinegar

2 tablespoons grenadine syrup

¼ cup pomegranate seeds

1. In large skillet, heat oil. Add onions, salt, and pepper; cover and cook 10 minutes, stirring occasionally.
2. Stir white wine, honey, vinegar, and grenadine syrup into onions; cook, uncovered, over low heat until onions are tender and all liquid evaporates, about 45 minutes, stirring occasionally.
3. Remove from heat; stir in pomegranate seeds. Spoon relish into jars. Seal and store in the refrigerator.

Honey Mustard *On the gift card for this sweet-and-spicy mustard, suggest serving it with sandwiches and smoked meats.*

Makes about 1¼ cups.

¾ cup Dijon mustard

¼ cup vegetable oil

¼ cup honey

2 tablespoons dry mustard

1. In 1-quart saucepan, heat all ingredients just until boiling, stirring constantly.
2. Remove from heat; cool and spoon mustard into jars or crocks. Seal and store in the refrigerator.

Cranberry-Kumquat Relish *Savor this refreshing mix with poultry and venison.*

Makes about 5 cups.

¾ cup honey

2 (4-inch) cinnamon sticks

2 tablespoons slivered crystallized ginger

1 cup seeded, sliced fresh kumquats

1 (12-ounce) package cranberries

1 (30-ounce) can pear halves, drained and each cut lengthwise in half

1 tablespoon lemon juice

1. In 4-quart saucepan, heat honey, cinnamon sticks, and ginger to boiling. Add kumquat slices, and simmer just until softened. With slotted spoon, remove kumquat slices and cinnamon sticks to small bowl. Discard cinnamon sticks.
2. Add cranberries to honey mixture remaining in saucepan. Cook berries just until they begin to burst; remove from heat. Stir in pears and lemon juice; cool.
3. Stir kumquat slices into cranberry mixture; spoon relish into jars. Seal and store in the refrigerator.

Apricot Spread *Slather this honeyed conserve on Christmas morning toast.*

Makes about 1½ cups.

1 (8-ounce) package dried apricots

¾ cup water

¼ cup honey

1 tablespoon orange juice

¼ teaspoon ground cinnamon

½ cup diced honeycomb with honey

1. In 2-quart saucepan, heat dried apricots and water to boiling over high heat. Reduce heat to low; cover mixture, and simmer apricots until very tender, about 15 minutes. Remove apricots from heat, and pour off

excess water. Stir honey, orange juice, and cinnamon into apricots.

2. In food processor with chopping blade, process apricot mixture just until almost smooth. Fold in diced honeycomb. Spoon apricot spread into jars; seal and store in the refrigerator.

Pinwheel Cookies *A prune-and-nut filling spirals inside these refrigerator cookies.*

Makes about 5 dozen.

2½ to 2¾ cups unsifted all-purpose flour

½ teaspoon baking soda

¼ teaspoon salt

⅓ cup butter, softened

⅓ cup sugar

1 large egg

½ cup honey

1 teaspoon lemon extract

Filling (recipe follows)

1. In medium-sized bowl, combine 2½ cups flour, baking soda, and salt; set flour mixture aside.

2. In large bowl, with electric mixer on medium speed, beat softened butter and sugar until mixture is light and fluffy. Beat egg, honey, and lemon extract into butter mixture.

3. Beat flour mixture gradually into butter mixture until soft dough forms. With spoon, stir in enough additional flour to make dough manageable. Wrap dough, and refrigerate several hours or overnight until well chilled.

4. While dough chills, prepare Filling.

5. To shape cookies, divide dough in half. On lightly floured surface, roll out half of dough to an 8-inch square, about ¼ inch thick. Spread half of Filling evenly over dough, leaving about ⅛ inch around edges uncovered with Filling. Roll up dough firmly, and press edge to seal, leaving ends open. Repeat with remaining half of dough and Filling. Wrap cookie rolls, and refrigerate several hours or overnight.

6. Heat oven to 350° F. Lightly grease 2 baking sheets. Cut rolls crosswise into ¼-inch-thick slices. Place cookie slices 1 inch apart on greased cookie sheets, and reshape slices into rounds. Bake cookies 10 to 12 minutes or until firm. Cool cookies on wire racks. Store in airtight containers.

Filling: In food processor with chopping blade, process 1½ cups walnuts until finely ground. Add ½ cup diced pitted prunes, ¼ cup sugar, 1 teaspoon ground cinnamon, 1 large egg, and 1 teaspoon grated orange rind; process until mixture forms a paste.

Christmas Cookies

The prettiest ornaments come straight from the oven.

Ribbon-threaded lady apples and gingerbread hearts enliven the tree (opposite) with the fragrance of fruit and spice.

A red-hatted gingerbread elf (above) dangles from a cedar branch.

Gingerbread Cookies

Makes about 18 (5-inch) cookies.

1¾ cups sugar

¾ cup honey

¼ cup butter or margarine

1 tablespoon grated lemon rind

⅓ cup lemon juice

6 cups unsifted all-purpose flour

¼ cup baking powder

⅛ teaspoon salt

1½ teaspoons ground ginger

1 teaspoon ground cinnamon

¼ teaspoon ground nutmeg

¼ teaspoon ground cloves

1 large egg, lightly beaten

1 egg yolk, lightly beaten

1. In 4-quart Dutch oven, combine sugar, honey, and butter; bring to a boil, stirring until sugar dissolves. Remove from heat; stir in rind and lemon juice. Cool.

2. Combine flour, baking powder, salt, ginger, cinnamon, nutmeg, and cloves. Stir 2 cups flour mixture, egg, and yolk into sugar mixture. Gradually mix in remaining flour mixture. Shape into ball; knead on floured surface until smooth. (Dough will appear dry before kneading.)

3. Divide dough in half. Roll 1 portion to about ¼-inch thickness on floured surface. Cut out with 5-inch gingerbread cutter or elf-shaped cutter; place on lightly greased cookie sheets. Cut a hole in top of each cookie, using a straw, if you want to hang cookies.

4. Heat oven to 325° F. Bake cookies 15 to 18 minutes or until golden; loosen with spatula, and cool 1 minute. Transfer to wire racks to cool. Repeat procedure with remaining dough. Decorate as desired; let dry.

Note: Avoid making these cookies during humid weather, or they may soften. Though edible, the cookies are very hard and are meant to be used as decorations.

A host of Angel Cookies hang from a Christmas tree encircled with gold ribbon and a garland of stars.

Angel and Ornament Cookies

Makes about 36 (6-inch) cookies.

½ cup (1 stick) butter, softened

¼ cup vegetable shortening

1¼ cups sugar

2 large eggs

3½ cups unsifted all-purpose flour

½ teaspoon baking powder

½ teaspoon salt

Angel and Ornament Patterns, pages 154—155

Royal Icing (recipe follows)

Yellow, burgundy, teal, and violet food coloring

Edible gold dust (optional; see note)

Small gold dragées (optional; see note)

1. In large bowl, with electric mixer on medium speed, beat butter and shortening. Add sugar; beat until light. Add eggs, 1 at a time, beating well after each addition.

2. In medium bowl, combine flour, baking powder, and salt. With mixer on low speed, add half of flour mixture to butter mixture; beat just until blended. Add remaining flour mixture; beat until soft dough forms. Shape into 3 equal balls; wrap and chill at least 30 minutes.

3. To cut out and bake cookies: Heat oven to 350° F. Lightly grease 2 cookie sheets. Cut 2 pieces of waxed paper the same size as cookie sheets. Lightly flour waxed paper, and roll out 1 ball of dough between paper to ⅛-inch thickness; keep remaining dough chilled. Remove top piece of waxed paper.

4. Using patterns, cut out cookies from rolled dough, leaving ½ inch between cutouts. Press trimmings together. Invert paper with cookies onto cookie sheet; peel off paper. Roll trimmings between paper; repeat cutting and inverting cookies to fill second cookie sheet. If making cookies to use as ornaments, use a toothpick to pierce a small hole about ½ inch from top of each cookie.

5. Bake cookies 8 to 10 minutes or until golden. Cool 5 minutes on cookie sheets, and then remove to wire racks. Cool completely before decorating. Repeat procedure with remaining balls of dough.

6. To decorate cookies, prepare Royal Icing. Divide icing in half, placing half in a medium bowl. Divide remaining half of icing among 3 small bowls. Using just a few drops of yellow food coloring, tint icing in medium bowl a very pale yellow. Mix 1 small bowl of icing with burgundy food coloring, another with teal food coloring, and last bowl of icing with violet food coloring (see note). Spoon icings (except yellow) into separate small pastry bags fitted with small (#1) tips.

7. Using pastry brush, paint front of each cookie with thin coat of tinted yellow icing, being sure not to cover pierced hole; let dry, and paint again. When icing has dried, brush angel cookies with gold dust, if desired. If using small gold dragées, place on angel cookies before icing dries. Pipe decorative designs on fronts of ornament cookies, using colored icings in pastry bags. If making cookies well in advance, store in airtight container, and freeze up to 1 month.

Royal Icing: In large bowl, with electric mixer on low speed, beat 2 (1-pound) packages confectioners' sugar, 6 large egg whites*, and 1 teaspoon cream of tartar until mixed. Increase speed to high, and beat icing until very thick and fluffy, about 6 minutes. Cover tightly with plastic wrap to prevent drying until ready to use. Makes 4 cups.

*Because uncooked eggs are not safe to eat, this icing is intended to be used for decoration. If icing is to be eaten, use 6 tablespoons meringue powder plus ¾ cup warm water, omitting egg whites; or follow meringue package instructions (see note) for Royal Icing.

Note: We used Wilton's meringue powder and egg yellow, burgundy, teal, and grape violet food colorings. Purchase wherever cake-decorating supplies are sold, or call Wilton Industries at (800) 772-7111.

White sugar angels
(top) and other cookie ornaments are made from the same traditional recipe.

Reminiscent of blown-glass ornaments that bedecked evergreens earlier this century, these sugar cookies are a fantasy in frosting (bottom).

Individually decorated sugar cookie hearts (below) are a traditional family Christmas project. To decorate a lot of cookies quickly, load colored frosting into a heavy-duty zip-top plastic bag. Snip off a lower corner and pipe away.

Hearts adorn this evergreen for Christmas (opposite). Together with strung popcorn, fresh cranberries, and tiny white lights, ribbon-tied sugar cookie hearts cloak this tree.

Baked lady apples,
lemon slices, and orange cartwheels
float atop a bowl of Golden Wassail.

Pleased as Punch

A cup of cheer before dinner warms the palate
as well as the heart.

Golden Wassail with Hot Buttered Apples
Old wassail recipes were concoctions of baked apples, ale, Madeira, and brandy. In this new version, applejack replaces a variety of spirits. Makes 20 servings.

1 gallon apple cider

4 (3-inch) cinnamon sticks

1 tablespoon whole cloves

1 whole nutmeg or 1 teaspoon whole allspice

½ cup orange juice

¼ cup lemon juice

1 large lemon, sliced

1 large orange, sliced

4 cups applejack

¼ cup firmly packed light brown sugar (optional)

Baked Lady Apples (recipe follows)

1. In a large stockpot, mix cider, cinnamon sticks, cloves, nutmeg, juices, and fruit slices.
2. Bring mixture to a boil over high heat. Reduce heat, and simmer 20 minutes.
3. Add applejack, and simmer 3 more minutes. Taste and add sugar, 1 tablespoon at a time, as desired to round off flavor.
4. Pour mixture into heated punch bowl (or leave in the pot), and gently ease Baked Lady Apples in to float on top.

Baked Lady Apples
Lady apples are the tiny golden variety with a pink blush that are available around Christmas. If you can't find them, substitute other small apples that weigh no more than four ounces each.

8 lady apples

8 teaspoons butter or margarine

4 teaspoons brown sugar

Ground nutmeg

Rum

Water

1. Heat oven to 350° F. Core apples to, but not through, bottoms, making as small a hole as possible.
2. Into center of each cored apple, put 1 teaspoon butter, ½ teaspoon sugar, a dash of ground nutmeg, and a drop of rum.
3. Place apples in a baking dish; add water to dish to depth of ¼ inch. Bake about 20 minutes or until apples are tender but not mushy.

Note: If you think some guests might enjoy a slightly more alcoholic beverage, set out a small pitcher of heated dark rum, adding about 1 tablespoon to each serving. A bowl of lightly sweetened whipped cream and a shaker of nutmeg are also nice touches that will turn the punch into Hot Apple Chantilly.

Spicy Wine Punch
This fragrant and fruity warm punch is best served in mugs. Makes 32 (1-cup) servings.

3 (1.5-liter) bottles dry red wine

3 cups dark seedless raisins

2 cups sugar

1½ cups chopped dried figs

3 (3-inch) cinnamon sticks

3 (½-inch-thick) slices fresh gingerroot

2 cups brandy

Clove-studded orange slices (optional; see note)

1. In nonaluminum 10-quart stockpot, combine wine, raisins, sugar, figs, cinnamon sticks, and gingerroot slices. Heat to simmering over medium-low heat, stirring until sugar dissolves. Simmer 15 minutes.
2. Remove wine mixture from heat; let stand 5 minutes. Remove and discard cinnamon sticks and gingerroot slices. Add brandy, and pour mixture into a heatproof serving bowl. Garnish with clove-studded orange slices, if desired.

Note: To make clove-studded orange slices, cut 1 navel orange crosswise into ¼-inch-thick slices. Discard end slices. Stud the rind of each slice with whole cloves.

Sparkling Christmas Punch *Cranberry juice and vodka are simmered with spices and then chilled and sparkled with soda.*

Makes 40 (1-cup) servings.

2 (3-inch) cinnamon sticks, crushed

1 teaspoon whole allspice

1 (5-inch-square) piece cheesecloth

Cotton string or twine

3 quarts apple cider

3 quarts cranberry juice cocktail

Juice of 3 oranges, strained

⅓ cup firmly packed light brown sugar

3 (1-liter) bottles club soda or seltzer, chilled

6 cups vodka, chilled

Cut-out apple slices (optional; see note)

Apple-cranberry garnishes (optional; see note)

1. Place cinnamon and allspice on cheesecloth. Pull up edges of cloth, and tie into bag with string or twine.

2. In nonaluminum 8-quart stockpot, combine cider, cranberry juice, orange juice, and brown sugar. Heat to simmering over medium-low heat, stirring until sugar dissolves. Add spice bag, and simmer 10 minutes. Remove from heat; cover and cool to room temperature. Refrigerate overnight.

3. Before serving, remove spice bag. Pour punch into serving bowl. Stir in club soda and vodka. Garnish with cut-out apple slices, if desired. Serve punch in mugs with apple-cranberry garnishes, if desired.

Note: To make cut-out apple slices and apple-cranberry garnishes, cut ¼-inch-thick slices from top to bottom of large green apples. Coat slices with lemon juice. With small star-shaped or other holiday cookie cutter, cut out center of each slice. Reserve the cut-out apple shapes. Float apple slices on top of punch. To make the garnish for each mug, thread a cranberry, the cut-out apple shape, and then another cranberry onto wooden skewer.

Sweet Endings

There's joy in making—and in
savoring—this most delicious part of Christmas.

Apple Charlotte *A charlotte (opposite) is a
shell of buttered bread that's filled with sautéed apples
and baked in a soufflé dish.*

Makes 12 servings.

**5 pounds McIntosh apples, peeled, cored, and thinly
   sliced**

1 cup (2 sticks) butter, divided

½ cup dark seedless raisins

¼ cup firmly packed light brown sugar

¼ cup water

1 teaspoon ground cinnamon

¼ teaspoon ground cloves

17 (½-inch-thick) slices firm white sandwich bread

Crème Anglaise (recipe follows)

Gold ribbon (optional)

1. Day before serving, in 5-quart saucepan, combine
apples, ¼ cup butter, raisins, brown sugar, water, cinnamon, and cloves over medium-low heat. Cook 45 to 55
minutes, stirring often, until mixture is the consistency
of thick, chunky applesauce. Cool to room temperature;
spoon into medium bowl. Cover and refrigerate at least
6 hours or overnight.

2. To assemble charlotte, in small saucepan over low
heat or in glass measuring cup in microwave, melt
remaining ¾ cup butter. Brush inside of 2½-quart
soufflé dish with butter. Trim crusts from bread slices.
Cut 15 bread slices crosswise into thirds, making 45
rectangles. With a 2¼-inch-round cookie cutter, cut
out 1 round each from remaining bread slices. Place
1 round in center of prepared soufflé dish. Arrange 12

bread rectangles pinwheel-style around center piece,
overlapping slightly to cover bottom of dish; brush
generously with butter.

3. Line side of dish with 20 bread rectangles, overlapping slightly to cover side of dish; brush generously
with butter.

4. Spread chilled apple mixture in bread-lined dish.
Place remaining bread round over apple mixture.
Arrange remaining bread rectangles around it pinwheel-
style, overlapping slightly to enclose filling. Brush with
butter.

5. Heat oven to 400° F. Bake charlotte 45 to 50 minutes
or until well browned. Meanwhile, prepare Crème
Anglaise. Let charlotte cool on wire rack 10 minutes.
Carefully invert soufflé dish onto serving plate; remove
dish, and let charlotte cool 15 minutes. If desired, tie
gold ribbon around charlotte. Serve with Crème
Anglaise.

Crème Anglaise: In 1-quart saucepan, combine
1½ cups milk, 3 tablespoons sugar, and 3 tablespoons
all-purpose flour, stirring until smooth. Heat to boiling
over medium heat, stirring constantly; cook 1 more
minute. In small bowl, using wire whisk, beat 1 large egg
until frothy. Gradually whisk in about one-fourth of
warm milk mixture; return egg mixture to remaining
milk mixture in saucepan, and cook, stirring constantly,
until a custard forms that will coat a spoon. Remove
from heat; stir in 1 teaspoon vanilla extract. Cool
custard to room temperature. Refrigerate custard,
uncovered, until ready to serve.

Gingerbread-and-Pear Tart *Wintertime favorites luxuriate in a creamy custard filling.*

Makes 8 servings.

4 cups water

1 cup sugar

1 (3-inch) cinnamon stick

4 (1½-pound) Bosc pears

5 tablespoons butter, softened

⅓ cup firmly packed light brown sugar

¼ cup molasses

1 large egg

1½ cups unsifted all-purpose four

1 teaspoon ground ginger

½ teaspoon baking soda

½ teaspoon ground cinnamon

½ teaspoon salt

Sour Cream Custard (recipe follows)

1 tablespoon apricot preserves or apple jelly, melted

Confectioners' sugar

1 long sprig fresh lemon thyme (optional)

1. In 2-quart saucepan, heat water, 1 cup sugar, and cinnamon stick to boiling over medium-high heat, stirring occasionally, until sugar dissolves. Meanwhile, peel pears; cut each lengthwise in half, and core.

2. Reduce heat to simmering, and add pear halves; cover mixture, and cook 10 minutes. Using slotted spoon, remove pear halves, and place, cut sides down, on paper towels to drain and to cool. (Poaching liquid can be refrigerated and used to poach other fruits, such as apples.)

3. Meanwhile, in large mixing bowl, with electric mixer on medium speed, beat butter and brown sugar until light and fluffy. Add molasses and egg, beating on high speed until smooth and well blended. Combine flour, ginger, baking soda, cinnamon, and salt; add to butter mixture, beating at low speed and scraping bowl as necessary until soft dough forms.

4. Heat oven to 375° F. Lightly grease a 10-inch tart pan with removable bottom. With floured fingers, press dough evenly over bottom and up side of tart pan. Place tart pan on a rimmed baking sheet; set aside.

5. Prepare Sour Cream Custard. Spread custard in bottom of dough-lined tart pan. With knife, score 4 lengthwise lines in rounded side of each pear half; place pear halves, scored sides up and stem ends toward center, in a ring in custard. Bake tart 30 to 35 minutes or until custard and crust are firm.

6. Remove tart from oven, and heat broiler. To brown pears on top of tart, cover tart with aluminum foil, pierce a hole in foil above each pear half, and pull back foil to uncover each pear only. (The foil will now look like a spoked-wheel stencil.) Brush pear tops with preserves; broil tart 1 to 1½ minutes or until pear tops are just browned. Remove foil, and cool to room temperature.

7. To serve, remove side of tart pan. Place tart on serving plate. Sift confectioners' sugar around edge of tart, and, if desired, garnish center with a sprig of lemon thyme that has been twisted into a wreath. Store any leftover tart in the refrigerator.

Sour Cream Custard: In food processor fitted with chopping blade or in blender, combine ½ cup sour cream, 1 large egg, 3 tablespoons sugar, 2 tablespoons all-purpose flour, 1 tablespoon milk, and 1 teaspoon grated lemon rind. Process or blend until smooth.

Cranberry-Orange Cake
A holiday classic gets a fresh twist with its jewel-like candied garnish.

Makes 12 servings.

3 large navel oranges

3½ cups unsifted all-purpose flour

1 tablespoon baking powder

½ teaspoon baking soda

½ teaspoon salt

1¼ cups sugar

1 cup (2 sticks) butter, softened

4 large eggs

1 teaspoon vanilla extract

1½ cups fresh or frozen cranberries, chopped

½ cup chopped walnuts

1 cup confectioners' sugar

Candied Orange Peel and Cranberries (optional; recipe follows)

Fresh mint sprigs and gold ribbon (optional)

1. Using a grater, finely grate rind from 1 orange, and set aside. If making Candied Orange Peel and Cranberries, remove orange part of peel in strips from remaining 2 oranges, using a vegetable peeler. Cut all oranges in half; ream in juicer, or squeeze to get about 1¼ cups juice. Set juice, grated rind, and orange rind strips aside.

2. Heat oven to 350° F. Grease and flour a 10-inch Turk's head mold or tube pan. In small bowl, combine flour, baking powder, baking soda, and salt.

3. In large bowl, with electric mixer on medium speed, beat sugar and butter until light and fluffy. Add eggs, 1 at a time, beating well after each addition. Beat in grated orange rind and vanilla until combined.

4. Reduce mixer speed to low, and alternately beat in flour mixture and 1 cup orange juice, beginning and ending with flour mixture, until batter is smooth. Fold cranberries and walnuts into batter; spoon batter into prepared pan.

5. Bake cake 55 to 60 minutes or until cake tester inserted into center of cake comes out clean. Cool cake in pan on wire rack 10 minutes. Remove from pan; cool completely on rack.

6. Meanwhile, in small bowl, with electric mixer or spoon, beat confectioners' sugar and 1 tablespoon orange juice until well mixed (icing should be smooth and just thick enough to drip from a spoon). If necessary, add more juice, 1 teaspoon at a time, to reach desired consistency. Prepare Candied Orange Peel and Cranberries, if desired.

7. Transfer cake to serving plate. Spoon icing over top of cake, allowing it to drip slowly down the side. If desired, top with candied peel and 5 cranberries; decorate with mint sprigs tied with gold ribbon and remaining 2 cranberries.

Candied Orange Peel and Cranberries:

Cut reserved orange peel strips into ⅛-inch-wide strips. Drop strips into small saucepan of boiling water, and cook 1 minute. Drain strips in strainer. Repeat with fresh boiling water to blanch orange strips again. Drain and return strips, plus 7 fresh or frozen cranberries, to saucepan. With fork, stir in 1 tablespoon sugar; heat until sugar dissolves and coats strips and cranberries. Cool to room temperature.

Chocolate-Cherry Torte

Follow each simple step, and you'll have this showstopping cake to show for your efforts.

Makes 10 servings.

1¼ cups dried sour cherries (see note)

1 cup water

¾ cup plus 3 tablespoons sugar, divided

1 tablespoon cornstarch

3 tablespoons Marsala, divided

1 teaspoon lemon juice

⅓ cup strong coffee

¼ cup boiling water

¼ cup unsweetened cocoa powder

⅓ cup vegetable shortening

2 large eggs

1 teaspoon vanilla extract

1¼ cups cake flour

½ teaspoon salt

½ teaspoon baking powder

¼ teaspoon baking soda

6 tablespoons buttermilk

1 (8-ounce) package cream cheese, softened

½ cup confectioners' sugar

1 cup (½ pint) heavy cream

Chocolate Meringue Twigs (recipe follows)

56 inches decorative ribbon (optional)

Fresh cherries (optional)

1. In small saucepan, combine dried cherries, 1 cup water, and 2 tablespoons sugar. Heat to boiling over high heat; reduce heat to low, and simmer until cherries are soft and liquid is reduced by half. Remove from heat. Transfer half of cherry mixture to blender or food processor fitted with chopping blade; process until a chunky puree forms. Return mixture to pan; add remaining dried cherry mixture. Add cornstarch, stirring until well blended. Heat mixture to boiling, stirring constantly; cook 1 minute, stirring constantly. Remove from heat; stir in 1 tablespoon Marsala and lemon juice. Cool to room temperature.

2. Combine coffee with 1 tablespoon sugar and remaining 2 tablespoons Marsala; set aside. In small bowl, stir boiling water and cocoa until smooth; cool to room temperature.

3. Heat oven to 350° F. Grease a 15- x 10- x 1-inch jellyroll pan, and line pan with waxed paper; grease and flour waxed paper. Set prepared pan aside.

4. In large bowl, with electric mixer at medium speed, beat remaining ¾ cup sugar and shortening until fluffy. Add eggs, 1 at a time, beating well after each addition. Beat in vanilla and cooled cocoa mixture.

5. Into small bowl, sift flour, salt, baking powder, and baking soda. Add flour mixture to shortening mixture alternately with buttermilk, beating until batter is smooth. Spread batter evenly in prepared pan; bake 18 to 20 minutes or until center springs back when gently pressed. Cool cake in pan on wire rack 10 minutes. Invert cake onto wire rack, remove waxed paper, and cool completely.

6. In large bowl, with electric mixer at medium speed, beat cream cheese and confectioners' sugar 2 minutes. In small bowl, beat cream until soft peaks form; fold whipped cream into cream cheese mixture just until blended. (Do not overmix.)

7. To assemble torte, using the bottom of a 9- x 5-inch loaf pan as a pattern, cut cake into 2 (9- x 5-inch) rectangles; use leftover cake trimmings as desired. Line the inside of the loaf pan with plastic wrap, allowing 2 inches to extend over the sides.

8. Place 1 cake rectangle in bottom of pan; brush generously with coffee mixture. Spread half of cream cheese mixture on top of cake in pan. Place another cake rectangle on filling; brush with coffee mixture, and top with cherry mixture. Place remaining cake layer on cherry mixture; brush with remaining coffee mixture, and top with remaining cream cheese mixture, spreading

smoothly. Cover torte with overhanging plastic wrap, and refrigerate at least 4 hours or overnight.

9. Prepare Chocolate Meringue Twigs.

10. To serve, remove torte from pan by pulling up plastic wrap on all sides. Place torte on serving plate; gently pull plastic wrap to remove. Press flat sides of chocolate twigs upright onto sides of torte to cover completely. If desired, tie ribbon around torte, ending with a bow in center of 1 long side. Top with fresh cherries, if desired, and serve immediately; or refrigerate up to 2 hours before serving. (Twigs will soften with refrigeration.)

Chocolate Meringue Twigs: Heat oven to 275° F. Line 2 large baking sheets with parchment paper (if not available, use aluminum foil, and grease lightly). Place ½ cup sugar and 2 large egg whites in medium bowl. Set bowl in a larger bowl of very hot, but not boiling, water. With electric mixer at high speed, beat mixture until thick and nearly doubled in volume. Remove bowl from hot water, and continue beating until stiff peaks form, about 4 minutes. Sift 2 tablespoons cocoa over meringue, and fold in just until blended. Transfer chocolate meringue to pastry bag fitted with a ⅜-inch round tip. Making narrow rows, pipe 3- to 4-inch strips of meringue onto baking sheets. Bake 1½ hours or until meringue twigs are dry and firm. Cool twigs completely on baking sheets on wire racks. Meanwhile, melt 1½ ounces bittersweet chocolate in microwave or in bowl set over simmering water. Dip fork in melted chocolate, and quickly drizzle chocolate back and forth across twigs, creating thin chocolate stripes. Refrigerate twigs just until chocolate stripes harden, about 5 minutes. Gently remove twigs from parchment, and store in airtight container at room temperature until ready to use.

Note: Dried cherries are available by mail from American Spoon Foods, 1668 Clarion Avenue, P.O. Box 566, Petosky, Michigan 49770-0566; (800) 222-5886.

Pistachio Semolina Shadow Cake

Semolina, the durum wheat flour that gives pasta its body, is the secret behind this moist cake.

Makes 12 servings.

4 large eggs

⅔ cup sugar

½ cup vegetable oil

¾ cup unsifted semolina (see note)

¾ cup unsifted all-purpose flour

1½ teaspoons baking powder

½ teaspoon salt

1 cup finely ground pistachios

1 teaspoon finely grated lemon rind

Syrup (recipe follows)

2 cups (1 pint) heavy cream

2 tablespoons confectioners' sugar

Sturdy piece of cardboard (optional)

1. Heat oven to 350° F. Grease 10-inch springform pan. In large bowl, with electric mixer on high speed, beat eggs and sugar until thick and pale, about 5 minutes. Reduce speed to low, and add oil, beating mixture until blended.

2. In a medium bowl, combine semolina, flour, baking powder, and salt; add to egg mixture, beating just until combined. Reserve 1 tablespoon ground pistachios; stir remaining pistachios and lemon rind into batter. Spread batter in prepared pan.

3. Bake cake 30 to 35 minutes or until golden and cake tester inserted in center comes out clean.

4. Prepare Syrup. With toothpick or skewer, randomly poke deep holes into hot cake in pan. Drizzle half of Syrup evenly over cake, allowing it to be absorbed; then pour remaining Syrup over cake. Set aside cake in pan to cool completely.

5. Just before serving, in large bowl, with electric mixer on medium speed, beat cream and confectioners' sugar until stiff peaks form. Using metal spatula, spread whipped cream evenly over cake, filling springform pan to top. Carefully remove rim of pan.

6. If desired, to make cake comb, cut cardboard into a 9- x 3-inch rectangle and also cut out a 1½-inch equilateral triangle to use as a stencil. Place 1 side of triangle stencil at end of a 9-inch side of rectangle; trace around it. Repeat this 5 times to make 6 side-by-side triangles on same long edge of rectangle. Cut out each triangle, creating comb-edged rectangle with 7 points.

7. Gently pull points of cake comb across cream on top of cake, creating peaks and valleys. Repeat combing several times to make deeper valleys, removing excess cream from comb each time. Reserve and refrigerate remaining cream for another purpose. Sprinkle reserved 1 tablespoon ground pistachios on 1 side of each peak. Place cake on serving plate. Serve immediately.

Syrup: In 1-quart saucepan, combine 2 cups water, 1 cup sugar, ¼ cup lemon juice, and 2 tablespoons honey; heat to boiling over high heat. Boil 10 minutes.

Note: Look for semolina in gourmet-food shops and natural-food stores. Two- and 5-pound bags of semolina are available from King Arthur Flour; to mail order, call (800) 827-6836.

Lemon Snowflake Cake *Lemon layers lie beneath a blanket of white chocolate snowflakes.*

Makes 12 servings.

Lemon Filling:

1 cup sugar

¼ cup cornstarch

¼ teaspoon salt

1 cup water

4 large egg yolks, lightly beaten

2 tablespoons butter

½ cup lemon juice

1 tablespoon finely grated lemon rind

Cake Layers:

3½ cups unsifted cake flour

4 teaspoons baking powder

½ teaspoons salt

2 cups sugar, divided

1 cup (2 sticks) butter, softened

1 tablespoon lemon juice

1 teaspoon finely grated lemon rind

1 teaspoon vanilla extract

1 cup milk

7 large egg whites

White Chocolate Snowflakes and Frosting:

4 (3-ounce) bars white chocolate, coarsely chopped

Silver dragées (optional, inedible)

1½ (8-ounce) packages cream cheese, softened

½ cup (1 stick) butter, softened

1 tablespoon lemon juice

1. Several hours or day before serving, prepare Lemon Filling: In 2-quart saucepan, combine sugar, cornstarch, and salt until well mixed. Gradually add water, stirring until smooth. Heat mixture to boiling over medium heat, stirring constantly with wire whisk; boil 1 minute. In small bowl, quickly stir some of hot mixture into egg yolks; then stir egg-yolk mixture into remaining hot mixture in saucepan until well blended. Reduce heat to low; add butter, and cook mixture 5 minutes, stirring occasionally. Remove from heat; stir in lemon juice and rind. Cool to room temperature; cover filling with plastic wrap, and refrigerate until filling is completely cold, at least 2 hours.

2. Prepare Cake Layers: Heat oven to 375° F. Grease 3 (9-inch) round cake pans, and line bottoms of pans with parchment or waxed paper; grease and flour parchment paper. In medium bowl, combine flour, baking powder, and salt.

3. In large bowl, with electric mixer at medium speed, beat 1¾ cups sugar and butter until very light and fluffy; beat in lemon juice, lemon rind, and vanilla. Add flour mixture alternately with milk to butter mixture, beginning and ending with flour mixture and beating until smooth batter forms.

4. In another bowl, with clean beaters and mixer at high speed, beat egg whites and remaining ¼ cup sugar until stiff peaks from. With rubber spatula, gently fold egg white mixture into batter. Divide batter evenly among prepared pans.

5. Bake 25 minutes or until cake tester inserted into center comes out clean. Cool in pans on wire racks 10 minutes; invert layers onto wire racks, remove parchment paper, and cool layers completely.

6. Prepare White Chocolate Snowflakes: In double boiler, over hot, but not boiling, water or in microwave, melt 1½ bars white chocolate into pastry bag fitted with writing tip. Reserve pan in which white chocolate was melted. Onto foil-lined sheet, pipe 28 (2-inch) snowflakes. Decorate with silver dragées, if desired. Place sheet of snowflakes in freezer until cake is completely frosted.

7. Prepare White Chocolate Frosting: Melt remaining 2½ bars white chocolate in reserved pan; set aside to cool to room temperature. In large bowl, with electric

mixer at medium speed, beat cream cheese until smooth. Gradually beat in melted white chocolate, softened butter, and lemon juice until frosting is smooth.

8. To assemble cake, trim tops of cake layers with sharp knife to make level. Place 1 cake layer on serving plate and spread with half of lemon filling; repeat with another cake layer and filling. Place last cake layer upside down on top of filling to make 3-layer cake. Frost cake smoothly with White Chocolate Frosting.

9. Remove snowflakes from freezer, and gently peel snowflakes from foil. Press a few snowflakes into side of cake; pile remaining on top of cake. Serve immediately, or store in refrigerator.

Patterns

Angel and Ornament Cookies

Recipes are on pages 130, 134-135.

All cookie patterns are full size.

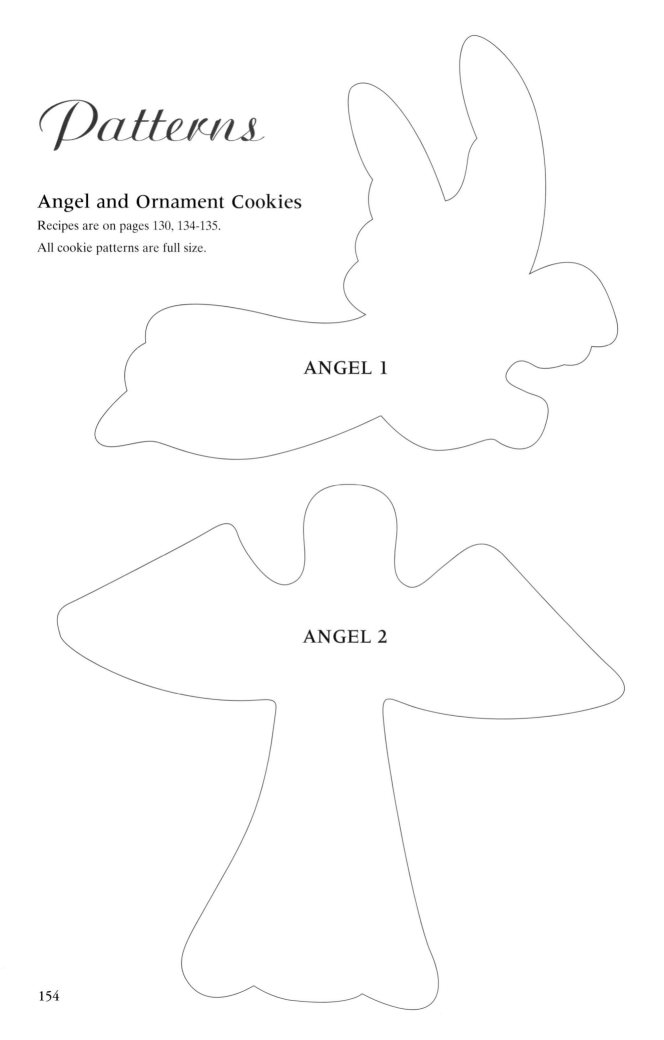

ANGEL 1

ANGEL 2

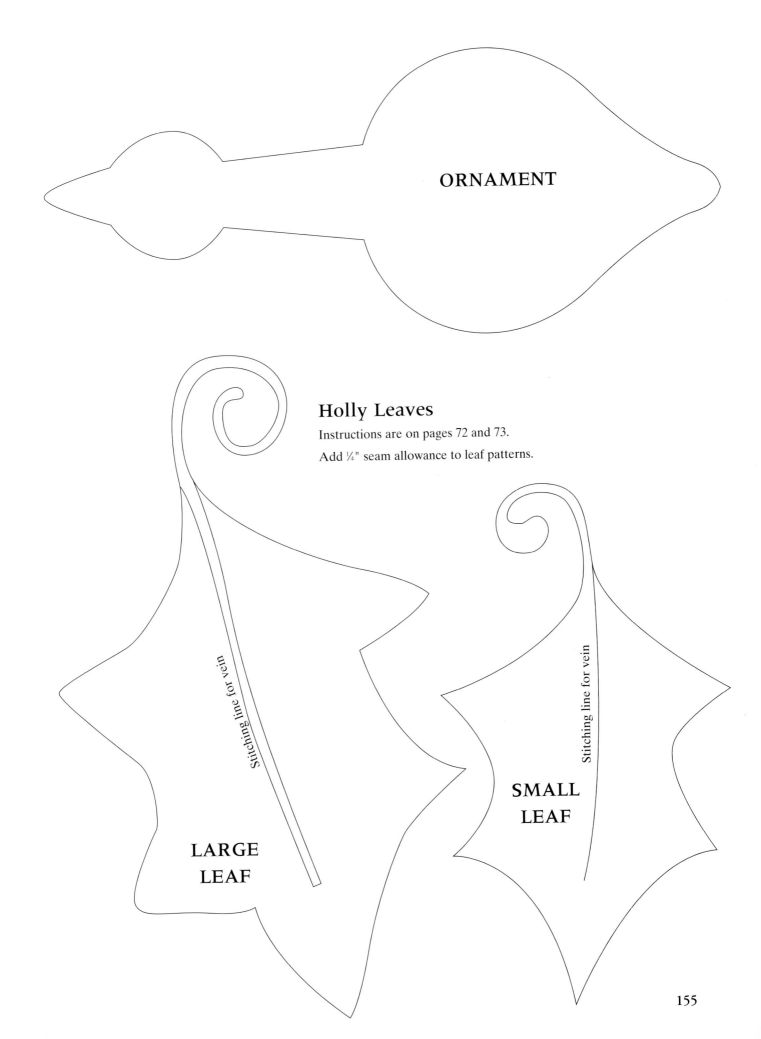

ORNAMENT

Holly Leaves

Instructions are on pages 72 and 73.

Add ¼" seam allowance to leaf patterns.

Stitching line for vein

LARGE
LEAF

Stitching line for vein

SMALL
LEAF

Holiday Stocking

Instructions are on pages 72.

Pattern is full size.

STOCKING

Align dots on stocking with dots on stocking toe to continue patterns.

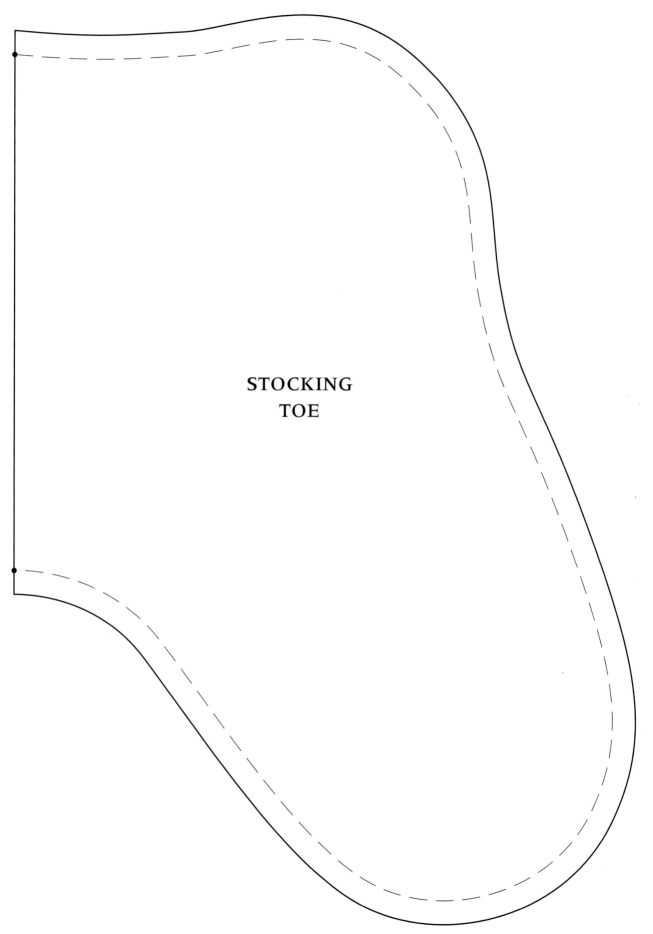

STOCKING
TOE

Contributors

Photographers

Jim Bathie cover, pages 1, 38, 39, 40, 41, 43

Feliciano pages 59, 108

Dennis Gottlieb pages 142, 145, 146, 149, 150, 153

Richard Jeffery pages 138-139, 141

Lynn Karlin page 65

Doug Kennedy page 35

Paul Kopelow pages 82-83, 94-95, 100-101, 102, 107, 136-137

Peter Margonelli pages 48-49, 82

Steven Mays pages 26, 42, 99

Keith Scott Morton pages 2, 10-11, 12-13, 14-15, 16, 17, 18-19, 20-21, 22, 24–25, 27, 28, 31, 32-33, 36-37, 44-45, 50-51, 52, 53, 54, 55, 56, 57, 58, 60-61, 64 (bottom), 66, 67, 68-69, 78, 79, 80, 81, 84–85, 90 (top right), 91, 96 (bottom), 103, 104–105, 106 (top), 110, 111, 112-113, 114, 115, 116, 117, 118, 119, 120-121, 128, 129, 132-133, 135

John O'Hagan pages 29, 64 (top), 70-72

William Stites pages 23, 46, 86-87

Jessie Walker pages 5, 6, 30, 34, 47, 62-63, 74, 75, 77, 90 (top left and bottom), 92–93, 96 (top), 98, 106 (bottom), 109, 122-123, 130-131, 157

Dale Wing pages 124-125, 127

Thanks

Kim Bealle

Susan Bellows

Rebecca Brennan

Kathy Diggins

Barzella Estle

David Graff

Jan Hanby

Ann Marie Harvey

Fran Reilly

Lisa Hooper Talley

Risa J. Turken